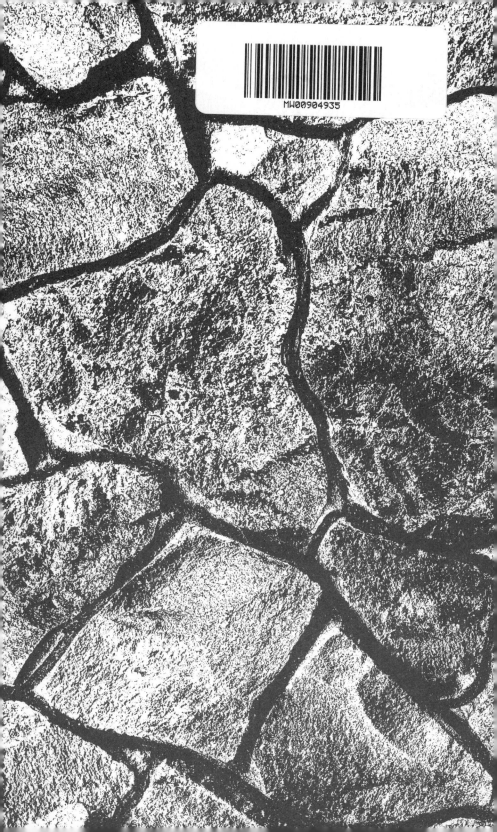

let us

not think

of them as

barbarians

LET US

POEMS

NOT THINK

OF THEM AS

BARBARIANS

PETER MIDGLEY

NeWest Press

Library and Archives Canada Cataloguing in Publication
Title: Let us not think of them as barbarians / Peter Midgley.
Names: Midgley, Peter, 1965– author.
Description: Series statement: Crow said poetry | Poems.
Identifiers: Canadiana (print) 20190075120 | Canadiana (ebook) 20190079037 | ISBN 9781988732664 (softcover) | ISBN 9781988732763 (epub) | ISBN 9781988732770 (Kindle)
Classification: LCC PS8626.I35 L48 2019 | DDC C811/.6—dc23

Board editor: Jenna Butler
Book design: Natalie Olsen, Kisscut Design
Cover texture © Ivan Popovych/shutterstock.com
Author photo: Myrl Coulter

NeWest Press acknowledges the Canada Council for the Arts, the Alberta Foundation for the Arts, and the Edmonton Arts Council for support of our publishing program. This project is funded in part by the Government of Canada. ¶ NeWest Press acknowledges that the land on which we operate is Treaty 6 territory and a traditional meeting ground and home for many Indigenous Peoples, including Cree, Saulteaux, Niitsitapi (Blackfoot), Métis, and Nakota Sioux.

#201, 8540–109 Street Edmonton, Alberta T6G 1E6
780.432.9427
NeWest Press www.newestpress.com

No bison were harmed in the making of this book.
Printed and bound in Canada 1 2 3 4 5 21 20 19

—koda:

…my hart is seer,

ons namibsroos is nie meer

you navigate the world differently after death
the woman thinks as she steps away from dragfoot

contents

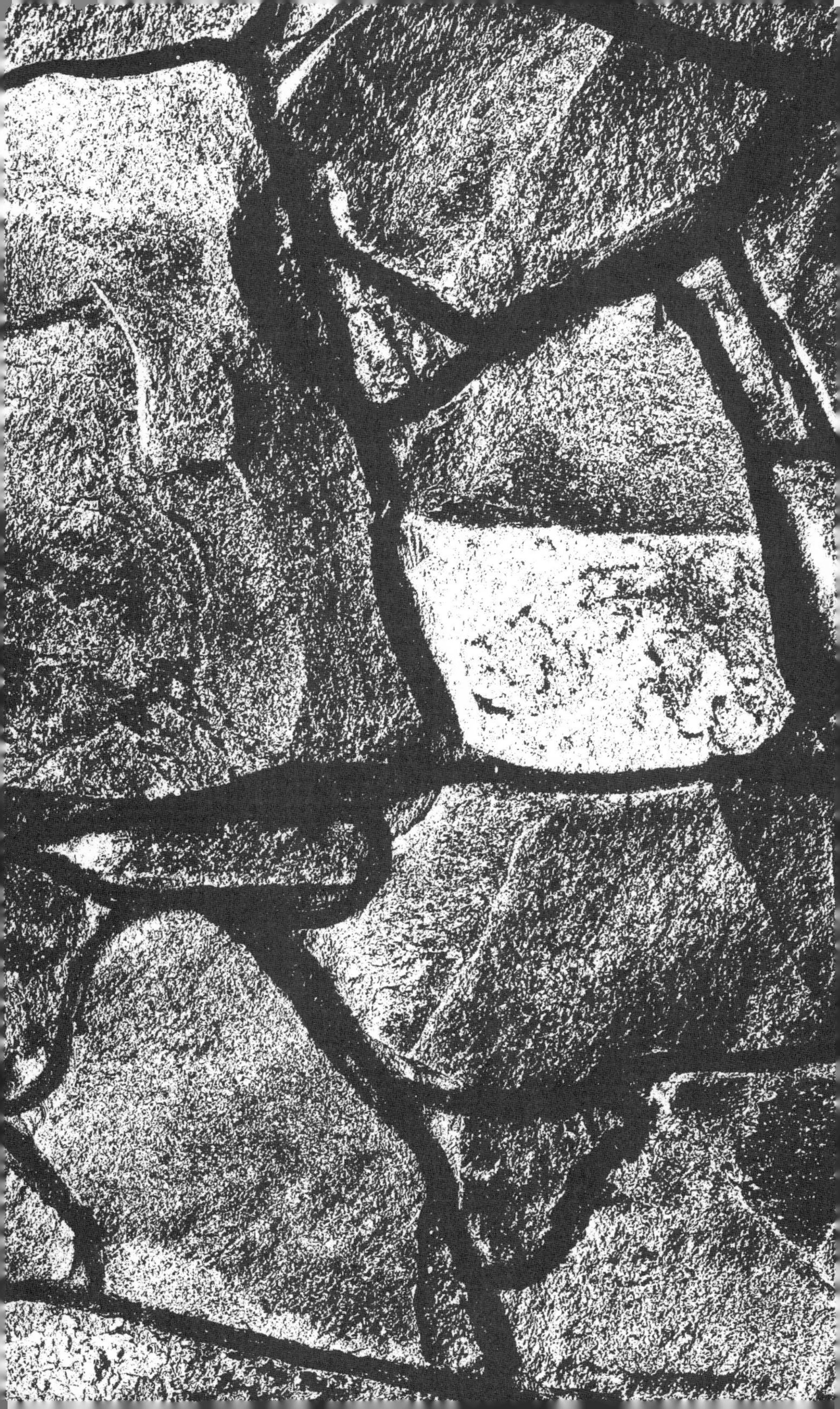

note

In 1904, war broke out between the Ovaherero of central Namibia, then known as German Southwest Africa, and the German colonists. On 1 October 1904, soon after the Battle of Ohamakari (Waterberg), the German general, Lothar von Trotha, gave his infamous *Vernichtungsbefehl*, or extermination order:

> I, the great general of the German soldiers, send this letter to the Hereros. The Hereros are German subjects no longer.... The Herero nation must now leave the country. If it refuses, I shall compel it to do so with the 'long tube' (cannon). Any Herero found inside the German frontier, with or without a gun or cattle, will be executed. I shall spare neither women nor children. I shall give the order to drive them away and fire on them. Such are my words to the Herero people.[1]

In a subsequent letter, he wrote, 'I believe that the nation as such should be annihilated, or, if this is not possible by tactical measures, expelled from the country.'[2]

His intent was clear, and thus began four years in which the Herero were systematically shot, rounded up, and placed in concentration camps. The labour camps at Shark Island off the coast at Lüderitz and at Swakopmund to the north served as death camps. Prisoners were worked to death offloading ships or building railroads into the interior. More than 90% of the prisoners on Shark Island died of exhaustion, hunger, and disease.

---

1 Qtd in Jan-Bart Gewald, 'The Great General of the Kasier,' *Botswana Notes and Records*, Vol. 26 (1994): 68.

2 Qtd in Mahmood Mamdani, *When Victims Become Killers: Colonialism, Nativism, and the Genocide in Rwanda* (Princeton UP, 2002), 11.

By the end of the war in 1908, only an estimated 12,000 Herero remained compared to the pre-war estimate of between 80,000 and 100,000. The Nama population fell from 20,000 to 2,000.

It was only in July 2016 that the German government agreed to acknowledge the events of 1904–08 as genocide.

In 1914, at the start of the First World War, South African troops were sent to expel the Germans; after the war, German Southwest Africa became a South African mandated territory under the League of Nations. Rather than lead the country toward independence, as required explicitly by the League's successor body, the United Nations, in UN Resolution 435, South Africa strengthened its control over the territory.

In December 1966, the first shots in the War for Independence were fired at Omugulugwombashe. For more than two decades, soldiers moved through the land and crossed its borders until, in 1988, a peace accord was signed at Mt. Etjo. This accord signalled the end of a colonial period that had begun four hundred years before that, when Bartholomeu Dias set a woman from West Africa ashore near Angra Pequeña (Lüderitz, as it is known today) in 1488.

Traces of this past can be found in the stories of the men and women who have wandered the land. Their stories gain power through retelling. Over time, specific dates and contexts disappear, rendering our modern linear conception of time obsolete. In such a world, ancestors march alongside us even as their names fade from memory. What remains is substance: the spirit of Mme Priskilla Tuhadeleni, who stayed behind when her husband, Eliaser, left to become a soldier. When he and his comrades crossed the border in stealth, they stayed at Mme Priskilla's house. When they left, she remained to face the wrath of the South African Defence Force and the Southwest African police.

What remains is the echoing footsteps of the Naro dancer who, in her words, danced the revolution 'with titties and soul.' And before them, Anna Mungunda, who ignited a revolution when she burned a police vehicle in Windhoek's Old Location. And even before that, the Woman of Dias, also known as the Guinea Woman, who was set ashore along the southern coast of Africa near Angra Pequeña (Lüderitz) on Dias's voyage around the Cape of Good Hope in 1488. We do not know what became of her, but she lives on through the dancers and the Mme Priskillas and the Anna Mungundas and the Herero women who chanted their defiant songs in the face of the German genocidaires. Women who rooted revolution in the land.

And as they remained, the men moved across borders — Danger Ashipala, Sam Nujoma, Rev. Michael Scott, Anton Lubowski. They left and returned, fighting for a place to belong. And so did the South African soldiers who crossed those same borders. And those who objected to the war. A rootless generation of wanderers.

In such a world, the only permanence is stone. The stone ramparts left by the South African forces along the Kunene River in northern Namibia; Klaas Afrikaner's stone fortress at ||Khauxa!nas in southern Namibia; an ancient hunting shelter along a Namib riverbed; the ramparts left by South African soldiers at Swartbooisdrif and at Dias Point — a reminder that the First World War was fought on southern African soil, too. And a stone's throw from Dias Point, where, in some ways, this story began, the stone burial circle lined with cowrie shells and the ombindi (cairns) that pay homage to the ancestors.

This is a story of stones. It is the story of the women who are the rocks that have taught the men to belong and to be strong, and who wear their khangas in defiance.

you cannot write these things down

you cannot write these things down
you cannot write them down
you cannot write them down
says the singer of praises.

the warm draft of summer
the burn of stone on bare feet
the blood of my rivers—

you cannot write this down
you cannot create calligraphies of pain
says the singer of sorrows.

an account of the herero

I.

have not the hereros been cattle-breeders ever since god created them?
as a cattle-breeder, does one not live in the selfsame way?
does one not live in the selfsame way when one is a cattle-breeder?

one treks with the herd wherever water and grazing can be found,
wherever grazing is to be found, one treks with the herd.
one treks with the herd in the selfsame way;
one follows in their manner:
wherever the herd treks, herero are to be found.

sometimes the cattle are stolen by our enemies.
sometimes they are stolen.
sometimes no thefts take place for years at a time.
sometimes the cattle increase and the people increase.
that is the life of omuherero: sometimes the cattle increase.

that was the life my great-grandfather lived.
that was the life my grandfather lived.
and my father lived it, too.
when we live exactly the same way,
there is not much to be told.

there is not much to be told, when one treks after the herd.
when one treks after the herd, *there is not much to be told.*
when people's tears fleck the omaheke, not much remains to be told.
wherever the bones of the herero are found,
the skeletons of the herd can be found.
there is not much to be told.

---

omuherero: An Herero person. The plural is 'Ovaherero' (The Herero people).

2.

listen for the songs of the ondjembo erose.
listen: the ondjembo will tell you where the cattle have moved.
listen for the ondjembo erose,
listen for the gut of the cow.
the ondjembo erose tells you where the herero are.
the cow gun that drives the cattle from one place to another
leads the herero. follow the ondjembo erose.
the ondjembo will lead you
to the bones of the ancestors.

listen to the ondjembo wail. listen to it wail in the wind.
listen to the omuhiva. listen to the wails.
listen to the songs of sorrow:
the bones of the herero. follow the bones
moving like a herd in the wind. follow the bones.
follow the ondjembo erose.

---

ondjembo erose: A horn (generally the horn of a gemsbok) used for herding cattle.

omuhiva: Commemorative Ovaherero and Ovambanderu oral performances.

3.

we learn to play the ondjembo
from our fathers. from our fathers we learn to play the ondjembo.
if our fathers are gone, the ondjembo is gone.
if the ondjembo erose is gone, the herds go too.
we cannot follow them.
we cannot follow them.
that is the way the herero live.
the herero cannot trek
where the cattle are not found.
if the grazing is gone, the herero are gone too.

sometimes the herero are stolen by their enemies.
sometimes they are stolen.
sometimes no thefts take place for years at a time.
sometimes the herero increase and their cattle increase too.
that is the life of omuherero.

the wind walks alone through the ondjembo erose.
the wind follows the bones.
the wind follows the bones of the herero.
wherever the bones are to be found
the herero are to be found.
beside poisoned wells,
wherever one treks,
the bones of the herero are found.

4.

have not the hereros been cattle-breeders since god created them?
as a cattle-breeder, does one not live in the selfsame way?
does one not live in the selfsame way when one is a cattle-breeder?

that was the life my great-grandfather lived,
that was the way my grandfather lived,
and my father lived it too.
when we live exactly the same way,
there is not much to be told.

let us not think of them as barbarians

i myself helped to kill one of them.

first we cut off his ears.
we cut off his ears. we cut them off.
we cut off his ears and whispered into them:
never again will you hear damara cattle lowing.
that's what we said as we cut off his ears.

we cut off his nose and we said to him:
never again will you smell,
never again will you smell damara oxen.
that's what we said when we cut off his nose.

we spoke these words to him as we cut off his lips.
as we cut off his lips, we spoke these words to him:
never again will you taste damara oxen.
that's what we said as we cut off his lips.

then we slit his throat.

dragfoot finds a body

dragfoot feels his way around the splayed body for secrets.
against the ramparts of her ribs each stone
and each cry lies bared. on this rosary he counts
every weal — those that came before and those still to come,
the gaping wound of his present:
with his hands he eyes every gap, rebuilds memory.

dragfoot reaches each stone into place,
in the present of her body he finds the eternity
of her hand as guide. dragfoot leans against the wall,
traces his fingers like a blind healer across her.
she traces her hand, the hand of a builder,
across each rock and each stone.
they feel the roughness of the earth
in their skin, in her hands.

they stack in haste,
hungry, without the careful measure and fit
of a mason. he feels her walls crumble;
she feels him flooding her.
she seeps into him.
her skin is rough against his.
her tongue laps against him
with knowledge.

a heart should not beat like this

for e.d. blodgett

a heart should not beat like this, not this loud,
the thrill of muscle dancing counterpoint to the body:
he rests his head on the pillow,
feels her muscles contract, his ears alive.

she sighs uneasily.
he reaches out his hand, feels her skin on his fingers
runs his hands over her wet body,
feels the stutter of her scars, feels her black body rising,
the growl of abrasive machines hollowing her veins —
hyenas foraging along the beach.

no heartbeat should echo this loud unless cut from its cage
it rages, rages, rages. cut from its cage it rattles and rages beneath him,
the clammy fingers of backhoes scraping her skin. and he cries.

in the bay, tankers hover, collect the black blood
oozing from her chest. black as dias's woman she is inside,
black as blood from these veins, black as woman.
he runs his fingers over her welts, reading their tender braille,
the effulgence of unseen words that roll like tumbrels from the sea.
he bends down, braids her hair into a necklace,
feels the texture of her hair against his skin,
smells the earth of it.

mopani seeds dance like butterflies from the trees
into waiting arms. he lays the tangled wings against her heart,
a necklace of seed and flesh and bark and skin,
skin and bark and flesh and seed.
a rampart of hearts against her tattered body.

he listens to the words mandume speaks to his mother,
he listens to them beat from her chest:
'take this necklace as a sign of my words, hang it against your body
hang it against your body in defiance of these guns that breed
horses of hunger: beware of the gifts they bring,
these hollowed horses that run through our land.
had i but lived a short while longer amid desert and stone,
had i but lived longer…'

                                                — oh, he dreams,
he dreams of tasting once more the wail of the antelope in the wind
of walking the verges of the world, of yelling at the skin of the soil.
he dreams of a gentler skin to clothe his naked body in.

                                          he trembles,
leaves her wet body and sets out:
a dragfoot man weaving along the road
clanging and swaying. an egyptian goose blares.
the muted bellman on the beach clings and clangs.
dragfoot stands alone. dragfoot spreads his wings,
a crippled goose stepping into the greying sky.

and then the seer's scream:
we keep the broken ones,
only the broken ones,
we keep only the broken ones
we gather at the edge of memory.
we keep the broken ones.

Mandume Ya Ndemufayo was the last king of the Kwanyama, who form part
of the Ovambo people of Northern Namibia. Ndemufayo reigned from 1911
to 1917, when he reportedly took his own life rather than submit to colonial rule.
Allegedly, as he lay dying, he took off his necklace and asked his aides to give
it to his mother as a symbol of continued resistance.

and drifting through the torment,
a hundred mouths and a hundred tongues:
the wounded, the crippled heroes, arms held high,
catch the mopani hearts that fall from the sky,
build a rampart, a chain of stone and bone and blood and vein
around and around and around her ribs.
fragile digits embrace the throbbing heart of the land.

in the snow and sleet of the desert, a single tulip
rises on the bared ramparts. dawn's khanga
flecks the horizon. birds gather at the feeder:
sparrows from the old world.
snow melts — tears of hope and sustenance
during the thawing of love
and above, above: terns   terns   damara terns marking their vigil.

there are two nights in this darkness where they lie side by side
with his outstretched hand pressing against her scars.
insects crawl in, spies from another world. settle on the lamp —
emissaries, harbingers, black as night.
the ants have left and the sky is grey.

their breath knits them to this frozen world.
they draw in the night:
a thousand eyes howling and mourning
and howling closer, ever closer,
sentinels guarding the pathway between worlds,
lovers tugged hither and thither between them:
a strange intimacy, this darkness before dawn.

---

khanga: The khanga is a colourful wrap-around garment originally from East
Africa, but now common throughout the continent.

words melt in his mouth

words melt in his throat, emerge dark as honey.
the night's clamminess ushers in the rattletrap dance of skeletons
against the horizon. they are legion, like the sands of the sea
and the skulls in the sand
the sailors   the explorers   the wanderers
the prisoners of this land.
they are legion. they are silent.

they have died in multiple ways,
each death a parting and a return.
who knows from whence they came.
what is departure? what is return?

taste the earth —
no, taste the earth,
go down on your hands and knees
dig down below the browned hide
to where the desert sand throbs a darkened red.
fill your fingernails with this soil, let it sink again black as honey,
this ink of my body, into the blotted desert.

taste the earth.
smell it.
feel it.
feel its textures and its joys
weeping to the surface
like water: the sorrow
the heartache
the bones of the ancestors
drying in poisoned wells.
taste this earth and feel its pain.
taste the earth
blotted with the ink of many bodies.

beyond the breakers

beyond the breakers, in the deep,
amidst rigs and fishing boats and seals
he looks back at the burning land:
he will take his leave.
he will leave this place and its hellish soil.
he will leave it,
leave it and its welts.

terns dart into the dappled nguni hide of the sea.
he hears the echo of her cries stitch the waves
together   turns, catches the wind
in his outstretched kaross,

washes up on the beach
a crippled traveller.

---

kaross: A skin rug or cloak used in southern Africa.

in the morning

birdsong at daybreak:
blackened monks curved between worlds,
reaching out beyond the waves
to steady this cantilevered earth.
here, at the edge of the world,
at the point where silence ends, the cry of terns
doubling back onto land: defying reason,
for who would willingly turn back to this,
except a dragfoot like him.

he feels it under his feet and in his bones.
no man should walk like this.
no man should walk like this,
his goose-neck cries at the terns' exuberant flight.

dragfoot lets go.

sometimes words do not speak to him

sometimes words do not speak to him.
sometimes the drought pervades his thoughts.
sometimes months pass this way and he withers—
yee-eh! the anguish!
the heartstopping breath!
where are they, these windswept words?
where are they, these bitter naras,
these fleshy, honeyed sounds
that rail against the frailness of the body?

they come with spring, settle like tumbrels against the desert rain:
gemsbuck searching for dew among the vygies spread red as words.

on and on and on and on and on and on these lines left breathless
settle into words.

---

nara: Acanthosicyos horridus is a species of melon endemic to Namibia.
vygies: Succulent ground cover of the subfamily Mesembryanthemoideae.

put a gun in my mouth

put a gun in my mouth.
put a gun in my mouth.
put a gun in my mouth,
i want to take aim.

put a gun in my mouth.
this gun that fought alongside mandume,
put it, put this gun
put it in my mouth.
put this gun in my mouth.

put mandume's gun in my mouth:
i want to fire with words
when bullets fail.

her shoulders rise like the hills

her shoulders rise before him
like hills of the auas mountains.
her breasts, the peaks of omukuruvaro
her thighs the mountain of the gods.
dragfoot circles her contusions,
circles the waist of this dark woman of dias.

dragfoot leans into the sounds of her body —
the throb of her heart drawing blood from the earth.

he draws his fingers over stone,
marks her welts as cracked visions.
the thirsty earth draws their water,
the thirsty earth draws them into itself like blood.

---

auas mountains: The Auas Mountains, located around the capital city of
Windhoek, are the highest mountain range in Namibia.

omukuruvaro: The Otjiherero name for the Brandberg Massif. It is a place
of great cultural significance and is rich in rock paintings. The name means
'Place of the Gods' in Otjiherero.

Little is known about Bartholoméu Dias or his trip around the southern tip of
Africa in 1488, and all we have to rely on is John Barros's account of the journey
in the Hakluyt Reports. Legend has it that Dias had on board four African women
who had been trained in contemporary European metaphysics and Portuguese
trading needs. Three of the women were dropped off north of Namibia and
charged with interacting with the locals to improve trade and to find out more
about Prester John. The last of the four women, so the stories go, was dropped
off near Angra Pequeña, or Lüderitz, as it is known today. Whether this is true,
or what subsequently happened to her, no one knows. She does reappear in
literature occasionally, notably as 'die donker vrou van dias' [dias's dark woman]
in the poetry of Antjie Krog (*Jerusalemgangers*, 1985).

the thirsty earth draws them. they throb,
their veins as black as the tarred streets of the city
on which she will dance her dance, the thundering reel
that welcomes sunrise over the mountains.

here, at the edge of their world,
in the flotsam and jetsam of their love
on the speckled nguni shores,
he casts his arm over her,
feels her ebb and flow.

dragfoot holds her close.
she is as brittle as the tides.
it is a fragile affair
this love of their bones.

she places her hands on his chest,
small butterfly mopanis
fluttering like terns on the beach.
she moves her wings
along his neck.
at his mouth, she pauses.
her fingers seek his tongue,
that flint of mandume's gun.

memory refuses to accept more faces

he enters her, feels the grip of her body
tighten around him in an almost forgotten memory.
she is slower and more generous than he recalls —
the dull ache of pain and memory,
the lost days of flesh against flesh.
he experiences her skin and her tawny caverns,
reads on the walls the lies of generations —
that absence caresses fondness
or that pain begets joy
and that land grows like desert
against the ebb and flow of the ocean.

here, dragfoot knows, you pray away the pain.
you pray and you pray until, tired beyond belief,
the lies emerge, washed clean. you pray for healing.

bowed in pieta before her body,
dragfoot prays away the faces that haunt his dreams,
the broken ones, the ones crushed by the desert sand.
he prays and prays until a pathway blooms pieta like a vygie
in the folds of her body, in the ebb and flow of the ocean.

the weight of airmail

it still surprises, the weight of airmail paper—
so delicate as if to drift on currents this news for her,
this declaration of love and lust and lives lost.
memory refuses to accept more faces—
how can it amidst the death and destruction?
what are we but an accumulation of miseries
and pain and indulgences begged from forgiving lovers,
their dead faces long receded? what remains is
this terrible news: of bombings and scars and lovers
among the quags silted over with bodies. it is too light,
this flimsy cage. it will tear and break. rain its sorrow on this land
on which her forebears crawled and dug and scraped and sweated
and bled their fingers to the nib. such cruel labour inhabits the blue:
words made to carry the weight of ancestral tears.

things that get lost

things that remain—
childhood photos;
family, books, friends;
inboxes, labelled, sorted, gone.

familiar things—
tongues to sing and bathe words in;
the warm draft of summer;
the burn of stone on your feet.

you can't write these things down.
you can't write them,
you can't write it down,
this ritteltit dance of freedom.
you cannot write it down.

dance, says the dancer of tradition,
dance a healing dance, a ritteltit dance,
dance the rattletrap dance of skeletons.
this dance of defiance, dance it with titties and soul.

the night's clamminess ushers in a string of black pearls
winding to camp against the desert horizon.
they are legion, like the sands of the sea
and the skulls in the sand   the sailors   the explorers
the wanderers and the prisoners.

the leaders   the pigs   the obscurants
numbskulls in the sand   idiots swarmed against the wind

dance the rattletrap dance of titties and soul
dance the history of dust
the grey stone of memory—
dance the rattletrap dance of remembrance.

the rain bulls of the khoekhoe

a pause   then the sky shudders
and breathes.
the sea crushes the stillness,
the perpetual absence of ants milling.

a train glides on the ribs of the dead,
each click and clack the snap of a skull.

the rain bulls of the khoekhoe grunt
and rumble like trains in the distance as they flee
before the horses, the iron horses of these people—
the ones the sea belched onto the beaches in anger.
the rain bulls bellow the anger of the desert.
they are dry bulls, uttering the drought—
weary cries that rattle the bones of the dead.

a child cries. her voice thin as the wind
blowing across the string of a goura.
she hungers even in death, this child.
shorn of all flesh, a reedy wail tumbles from her ribs,
asks for the return of the wet rain bulls,
the bulls of plenty, the bulls of harvest.
back and forth the delicate ondjembo of her voice
quavers across the desert, over the plains.

---

goura: The goura is a mouth-resonated bow. The string is attached to a quill
and stretched over a hard stick. To play the instrument, the player inhales
and exhales on the string, thus creating a resonant vibration that is has been
described as bird-like. Herdsmen among the Khoisan use the goura to give
instructions to their cattle.

the sands of the omaheke inked red with the wails of the children
draw a kaross over the woman, the unfortunate one,
the sleeping one. the sand draws a veil of sand over her
and the body beside her, the dragfoot man who hums
songs of love, of war.

the throb of the horses
serves as lullaby,
the thrum of horses
doubles as heartbeat.
the clop of the rain bulls
doubles as heartbeat.
the erratic rattle of bones
doubles as heartbeat.
their blood stills in the sand.
in the stench of rotting flesh,
their cries still like blood.

in the flailing seconds before he wakes,
in that infinitesimal void,
gasping for breath,
wakefulness comes suddenly.
life eases back into dragfoot with a shudder—
heartbeats on stone
numbed from the cold of the night.

---

omaheke: The Herero name for the Kalahari Desert.

a man walks out of the mountain

a man walks out of the mountain
carved from the rock and dust of these mines:
a whitened onganga dances the centuries,
a whitened onganga dances the bones.

those who came riding, riding,
those who came riding their horses
and their stomachs of wind,
they are blown like german pom-poms
across the omaheke — they, too, tasted exile,
felt the tears of the desert
in their bones.

a song emerges
from the night:
how can we cry
when we cannot mourn our dead?
the tails of our cattle lie scattered,
as many as these sands.
taste their blood, taste,
for they are legion
these sands and these tales adrift in the desert.

---

onganga: A traditional healer.

dragfoot dreams of joining the hunt

hungry for words, dragfoot slavers before the shelves of the city,
laps up each sensuous detail with the zeal of a hound giving tongue.
he breaks cover, dwells amidst the pages of the ancestors.
he marvels at the welts that have risen on his body.
to fall under such inquisition is holy, he thinks.
he casts himself on the ground,
becomes one with his god.
he wakes and checks himself:
it is sinful to cavort in this babble of blank words.
the welts of earthly tongues bruise his body,
tattoo his thoughts onto his skin.
dragfoot fasts for his god; yearns for the flesh
of things other than the books of men.

he is of two bodies: consumed by desire
he feeds on the perfection of the tongue.
in time, he honours a different line,
follows the scent of words on the page like dogs at the races.

song of the herero

and as the last footfall recedes in the dusk, she starts to unfurl
from the earth: ahead lies the night,
row upon row of footsteps cross-stitch across the thorns,
pluck at the veins, knot a ball of sinew and sweat:
day dries the night to indivisible mass,
clots it to resistance.

von trotha's *groot rohr* treks by night and by day
slowly and slowly the rasp of its wheels on the frost
and the wind, oh god, the wind in the night
and the yoke on your shoulder: how awkward the earth
and the shuddering bodies huddled against you — too tired
to fight any more
too tired to provide heat.
we plod along
with child and sack and beast,
half dead.

and so we trek
in search of water,
that body of water along the border,
the water that protects
against the darkness of the *deutsche rohr*.
far in the night the wheezing cry of herero blood.
the ondjembo song tramps pathways of hope:
the children will sing omutando that rumble
the tails of cows that lie lost
in wells of blood.

---

groot rohr / deutsche rohr: Big gun/cannon.

omutando: Ovaherero praise songs.

we forge ahead
drinking the blood of man and beast
in our communion of dread.
imagination creates its own gravity: the weighing of planets
suspended like spider shadows in the early morning sun,
thinner than the railed spines of our children's breath.

as the first rays of sunlight heave through the mountains
she leans against me in the dusk of a donga.
hidden here, we can rest up for another night.

my bony fingers slide down her ribs:
the bulge of her stomach kicks with hunger —
no hope for the future in this abacus
on which we compute only our dead.

---

donga: Gully or gulch.

his feet scarcely enveloped by his sandals

the gentle earth crumbles underfoot
as he turns to his lover and speaks:
how do you slay demons?
stone is not a dead thing.
stone has life.
stone is a spirited thing.

how does one carry a world in one's head?
i have died in multiple ways,
like stone.
each death a parting and a return.

in the sands of the omaheke,
on the shores of the namib,
at the ramparts of the kunene,
dragfoot speaks to his lover:
i have died in multiple ways,
arriving and leaving the blink of an eye.
i have died multiple deaths.

.

kunene: The Kunene River has its source in Angola and runs to the Atlantic ocean,
forming part Namibia's northern border.

a history of dust

this ink of my body, bleached into the desert—
taste it: taste this ink and this earth.
go on your hands and knees,
fold your hands in supplication under the browned hide
where the desert sand throbs a darkened red.
with your soiled fingernails, red monk, utter a prayer
of the desert. squat like a succulent on the ramparts of the land,
bleed words and taste the earth, the red oil seeping through your lips.

smell it. smell the salty blood of your words.
feel the earth, its textures and its joys weeping in your mouth,
mingling with your blood.
taste its sorrows, its heartache.
hear the rattling bones of the ancestors in poisoned wells.
taste this earth saturated with the ink of many bodies.
taste this history of dust.

rise up and dance, says the dancer of tradition. dance
a healing dance, a ritteltit dance.
dance the rattletrap dance of skeletons.
the night's clamminess lays down a string of blackened beads,
bared bodies lashed to the desert.
they are legion, like the sands of the sea and the skulls in the sand,
the sailors and the explorers, the prisoners of war:
dance a rattletrap dance for them.
plant your feet in this parched soil:

oh god!

red as a grenade this pomegranate in my hand,
this ball of blood and dust and bone
pulsing and raw as my love for this land,
my love   my dripping pomegranate: we dance
love's bloody waltz along the knuckled syntax of your bones
the beat of dido dido dido dying in carthage
the bodies of el alamein and cassinga and ohamakari.

Dido: According to legend, Dido was the first queen of Carthage, who fell in
love with Aeneas. When Aeneas betrayed her love and left Carthage, she killed
herself. Dido resurfaces in Ovid and again in Dante's *Divine Comedy*.

Carthage: The Capital of the Carthaginian Empire.

El Alamein: The Second Battle of El Alamein (23 October–11 November 1942)
was a key battle during the African Campaign. Soldiers from southern Africa and
Namibia were deployed as part of the Eighth Army.

Cassinga: On 4 May 1978, South African forces attacked the South West African
People's Organisation at Cassinga in Angola. The attack remains controversial
because of contesting claims as to whether it was a military base or a refugee camp.

Ohamakari: The Battle of Ohamakari (Waterberg) broke out on 11 August 1904
between the Ovaherero and German imperial armed forces. The defeated
Ovaherero retreated into the desert, where they died of thirst and starvation.
Only a few reached safety across the border in the British Protectorate of
Bechuanaland (modern-day Botswana). It was after this battle that General von
Trotha gave his *Vernichtungsbefehl* that sanctioned the genocide.

the bones become a refuge

they will come and they will go as the tides
ebb and flow   as the desert beats
against the banks of the kuiseb
white as skeletons
white as the hairs
on the heads of ovahona.

sadness calcifies the army   bodies whitened in the rust:
taste it   taste the rust of the earth and the bodies,
taste the corrosion of words that grow like ancient planets
on your lips. hear the supple earth groan and bend.
our feet leave a wounded calligraphy
that sings revolution in the mist.
the screams impaled on the sun weep and blossom
like the skulls and the brittle shells caught in the corrosion of tides —
alluvial glitter: thus a nation is born
from recalcitrant thighs.
and the terns   damara terns   reaching out from the edge
swoop and dart a pattern of words:
how their tongues have keeled in foreignness.

this is living, dragfoot thinks.
his body has fled with the terns and the tides,
sought refuge from itself. in the desert,
among the ramparts, he forages in the sand,
devours hunger.   his stomach overflows.
dragfoot retches a dream from which there is no waking:

---

kuiseb: The ephemeral Kuiseb River flows from the Khomas highlands west
of Windhoek to Walvis Bay.

ovahona: Ovaherero elders.

vultures feed on the bones of the ocean.
each rattling intake of air,
each skull of an ancestor, shimmers in the dew,
a standard leading the battle against breath.

let us wake from this lurid dream
where the women march through the wraiths they birthed
and the skulls they steamed.   let us live
my love, and let us lie together in this ochre blanket.
let your trembling body settle beside mine,
let us rattle and sway to the rhythm of ghosts
in the hollows of our bones.

the horses of hunger

we ride the horses of hunger
the horses of hunger, we ride them
the horses of hunger
we ride them on stomachs of air.

smoke curls from the nostrils of dragons.
flared in anger their breath smoulders.
ah, these horses, these horses of hunger,
their breath smoulders in empty stomachs,
fulminates as it leaves the body:

>   put a gun in my mouth
>   put a gun in my mouth so i can take aim.
>   put a gun in my mouth,
>   this gun with which i fought
>   alongside mandume,
>   put it, put the gun
>   put the gun in my mouth.
>
>   put mandume's gun in my mouth.
>   i want to fire with words
>   when bullets forsake me.

the earth needs a pacemaker

the earth needs a pacemaker,
a two-stroke lister to pump pure blood:
to the north there's water underground and the heart draws
deep, close to the earth's warm skeleton.
yet dragfoot avoids the vein,
aims for the southern bypass:
thus we write around history.

the dragfoot man leaves the trail

the dragfoot man leaves the trail like a snake in the desert.
the dragfoot man writhes his feet into the sand,
lives close to the earth. and beside him a woman,
black as the fences of the camp, dances.
she sings out the silence: the walls of the city
branded and barred.
the woman dances her dance of defiance,
a ritteltit dance, an undanced dance of generations
falling to the beat of bombs and the footfall of guards
and the children leaving and returning,
returning and leaving in the wail of the tide.

the woman dances to the sound of the ondjembo.
the woman dances a silent dance, a dissonant dance,
the dance of the desert woven into the hands of her dragfoot man.
she holds his hands. together, their hands have seen battle,
written words of nothingness, words of iron,
words like railroad tracks on which trains thunder
like rain bulls bearing the bounty of the land:
a multiplicity of voices
a multiplicity of witnesses
a multiplicity of bodies —
debris of this revolution of the heart.

her hands unfold like the lines on the shores.
in the red of the desert, in the blackness of the bloodied streets,
she draws their love in the midday sun. he reaches beneath the heat
for the safety of the evening. he moves slowly
into the night as it casts its kaross over the truth
of their bodies. hidden in darkness, they are one. they are safe.

her heart is desert rose

her heart is desert rose,
hoodia crumbled to dust
by sea and sand.

skin dark parchment
bleached by the winter sun.

bones pounded against the desert sand
barbarically exposed to blade:
silver canes under this geography click
against the contours of bearing bone.

her heart is brittle desert,
stuttering pump that leaks words
through dry furrows,
frail as tumbrels beating against ribbed cage.

the braille of a lifetime's scars —
a century of short circuits
between brain and bone.

new couplings curse and curve
through the brittle frame that refuses
to return to dust.

---

hoodia: Hoodia, known colloquially as the desert rose, is a medicinal desert plant.

the woman's heart is stone and stain

the woman's hand is stone and stain,
brown as the earth from which it blooms.
the woman seamed to the dilapidated fence
of the camp greys against water and stone.

the one born out of violence of this earth
dances in the streets,
runs her hands through the filigree of her voice:
she is wound around herself as the strings of a heart
are wound around the body, enclosed in welts
like the mountains and the valleys of her pain:
a heart that bleeds, bleeds good and well.

her kaross slips from her shoulders in the morning,
falls on the sand in the forest of salt and stone.
she draws him in, this child of lot,
her dragfoot lover.
she draws him into her heart,
pumps him through the black veins
that thump with the thunder
of thousands upon thousands upon thousands
of hooves. a surfeit of people, a surfeit of dead,
a glut of bones piled up
waiting to take flight.
in this land of stone and bone
they wander entwined, two vagrant lovers.

press a hand in my gentled bed

press a hand in my gentled river bed,
this tattered kaross of a night sky
drawn across my thighs.

we move from bay to bay,
from point to point.
we gather bodies like flotsam in the tide —
back and forth, back and forth
like silt on the shore,
like bodies in the shallow bay.

dragfoot can't get it out of his head, the south.
falcons circle this place.
remnants of crops remain
in their stone cages,
the blisters of those days.

shark island

Sie! said the kommandant.

and you and you and you and you and you and you and you
and you and you and you and you and you and you
und du und du und du und du und du und du
en jy en jy en jy en jy en jy en jy en jy
und du du du du du du du du du

und Sie

Sie Sie Sie.

vierzigmal.
und dann noch fünf.
und dann nichts mehr.

forty-five skulls is all they needed
in the curio shops of europe.

after all, they were not barbarians.

Sie / du / jy: you.
vierzigmal: forty times.
und dann noch fünf: and then five more.
und dann nichts mehr: and then no more.

christmas (building the railroad)

one, two, three
one, two, three
five times over,
in groups of three
and then some more.

that is how many died on that day
laying track as they listened to the kommandant read
the word of god at the end
of a season of peace and goodwill.

after all, they were not barbarians.

the germans need to sit down

the germans need to sit down.
there's no place for their horse here.
in berlin for sure. there's a place for a horse in berlin,
but not here! not here! there is no place for that horse here.
let the *reiter* take his horse back to germany;
let us bring our remains back home.
the germans need to sit down.
we will take the horse off its pedestal.
we will take it down. it is in the wrong place.
the germans can take their horse back to germany,
there is no place for it here.

---

reiter: equestrian, horse rider.
The *Reiterdenkmal*, or Equestrian Monument, was erected in 1912 outside
the Alte Feste — the Old Fort — in Windhoek to commemorate the German
soldiers who died in the Wars of Resistance. It has been the subject of much
controversy, and is currently in storage at the Alte Feste.

horses at garub

in the winter sun of garub,
horses crowd the car, then stand motionless
to lick the salt—a harmony of tongues reaching
through silence as if this saline gift were an apple
proffered by some majestic hand.
the listless horses stand, the cries of their kaiser
long departed; proud german martingales
exchanged for the wild snaffle of a desert wind.
children of lot, they toss their shaggy manes
and turn their backs to the wind. and stand,
eyes shuttered against the stark yellowed dunes,
as if rooted in this foreign sand.
what frugal stubble drew them here,
and now feeds these hundred haunted manes?
surely the plains of garub gave them birth.
abandoned by fleeing riders, yet they chose to remain
and grow again, rooted now in alien land.
a horse of the garub, i've been told,
can hear the footfall of the dead
and the jingle of a soldier's bandolier
and the ceaseless songs of praise.
but when a ghost emerges from the mist,
they stop dead where terns blown in from the sea
flutter and dart above the railway tracks.

---

garub: The Garub Plains near Aus in Namibia's Namib-Naukluft National Park
are home to a feral herd descended from the German cavalry horses abandoned
during the First World War. Although they are an exotic species, they are allowed
to live within the bounds of the Park and are considered an important part of
the cultural heritage of the country. In 1992, during a severe drought, the Garub
Horse Project built a permanent water source at Garub.

then amid that boisterous dancing in the skies
these abandoned beasts whinny to the wind
and with slow, deliberate unison
bend their heads to the ground
to hear the voices echoing from the deep:
'ehi rovaherero, ehi rovaherero'
the faded bones chant to the desert wind.
and at the sound of this ancestral lament
the horses of the garub reach across stormy seas
and let their desert threnodies whinny home
those dreadful bones in europe's vaults.
visitors to these desolate troughs
standing sentinel in the plains of garub
should heed the deferent human hand
that drew water from beneath the sand
and built at garub walls of stone to slake
the salted-encrusted statues of stubble
who years ago outran the kaiser's crop
and turned their backs on ocean spray.
now, huddled together in the wintry sun,
they bow their heads towards the earth,
and stand. thus in solidarity
alien man and beast pay homage,
show their kinship to this land.

---

ehi rovaherero: 'This land belongs to the Ovaherero!' During the
Wars of Resistance (1904–08), Herero women chanted these words
as encouragement to soldiers on the battlefield.

this crippled goose

he stumbles to the shore, this crippled goose
with his hunched shoulders and gimpy leg. stands passively,
body askew, face drooped into solemnity, or fatigue,
like his shoulders. thus he stands, this wounded warrior,
his voice rising querulously, as if stuttering through the welts
of his heart, and hers. dragfoot clangs the tenuous flight of terns
over the horizon, scanning the shoreline for her, his earth-bound lover.

he walks humbly among the ruins of his troubled heart.
his voice grows like the continent from which it rises
as she dances into sight, dancing her unfinished dance of freedom
on the steps of the shebeen, her blood flowing like beer
onto the blackened streets: this is freedom. this is love.
it rises from the wars and the bodies that embrace them,
clots to pools of blackened blood like oases in the desert.

---

shebeen: Illegal drinking house.

petrel at daybreak

blood from the eyes of the woman runs like tears:
birdsong in the morning, a canticle of black monks
curving their cauls between earth and sky,
steadying this cantilevered earth.

behind him, incessant footfall has tamped the earth,
left a mocking echo of the sky's guinea-fowl breast
at the edge of the world. here, silence ends.
here, the cry of a single tern doubles back onto land.

a woman stands on the beach. her hand is stone and stain,
brown as the earth from which it bloomed. her veins
string like dilapidated fences along the waterfront,
greying against sand and water
and desert stone.
                             he turns away,
his body glistening in the naked morning sun.
his boat lies desolate on the beach at messemb bay.

he turns back, pushes the bowsprit into the water, cleaves the waves,
runs the skiff's barnacled tongue across foaming breakers.
in the deep, amidst rigs and fishing boats and seals, a petrel hovers
black and rising out of sight as he approaches,
playing hide and seek, elusive as a lover
blown in by some storm. curiosity awakens the mist
on the shore. it gathers around the woman's bones,
larger than expectation. ahead, the petrel's eyes
discernable only as limpets glistening.

---

messemb bay: A small inlet in Griffiths Bay just south of Lüderitz.

you navigate the world differently

you navigate the world differently after death,
the woman thinks as she steps away from dragfoot.
they have recited the canticles of the body
in their liturgy of dawn; offered last rites to the night.
now, at the rouse, he lies on the ground in holy state,
as if one with the earth. she is restless as the morning air.
she wraps dawn's yellow khanga around her waist,
gathers her kaross and sets out to follow the herd,
the herd fattened on the grass of their bodies
and the mist harvested from the night.

she steps away from dragfoot and follows the herd
toward the camp. she follows the herd and her heart bellows
at the dawn, for she has tasted pain in the sand.
her broken cries taunt the valley
and the starved cattle of the rain echo her laments.
she follows the mottled necklace of the herd
over horizons. she follows the herd.
in her heart, she is troubled,
calls deep to deep across the continent,
asks for a revolution of the tongue.

she has fallen in love with this dragfoot creature,
with his clanging bells and his necklace of bullets
gathered from war. he is shackled by the pain he has seen,
and she weeps for him. she weeps raindrops of longing,
and the rain bulls cast a blanket of tears over her.
she walks slowly in her dazzling khanga,
taking with her the remaining wetness
from the hide of the earth.
                              he is shackled,

yet she envies him the security of this earth
to which he is bound.

                      she moves between worlds,
takes on the pain of generations in realms of stone.
the earth anchors him.

she follows the herd over the horizon.
she follows the herd to the camp.
she sews the death of the rain bulls
onto the desert fences.
she sews the trains that emerge from the coast,
the iron bulls that usher in pestilence,
she sews these bulls to the revolution of her heart.
there is little to be told: the cattle in the kraals increase
and the dead increase. their bones clack
along the abacus of death, inland and out.
the narrow spine rattles with death
and the cry of starving rain bulls.
she envies dragfoot the peace of his shackles.

she follows the trains of soldiers crossing the kunene.
she follows the trains of his people as they follow the soldiers.
she follows the trains like she follows the herds.
she watches the horses of hunger parade through the land.
she numbs her senses to the numbness of knowing.

and under the kaross,
dragfoot hauls himself from the mud of her absence,
takes on the shape of the day. he stifles a crippled cry
at the sight of the broken ones,
the skeletons that thorn the path under her feet:

---

kraals: Enclosures for cattle; corrals.

they have marched through the dawn,
they have marched through the horizon,
across the kunene. they have slunk
through the night like prayers in the mist,
their eyes raw and their words
the hesitant footfall of troops.
in the early morning light,
they dance a rattletrap dance of rib and bone.
And, ee-eeh, the wind! the wind of the night
clings to his body. the wind of the night seeps the thin
reel of the morning through his body: thus
the revolution of the heart turns
on its delicate axis.

he will husband only bones now in these fields of red —
the crop of his father and of his father's father before him.
he will grow bones from the remnants of passion,
bones from which to build a skeleton,
an abacus on which to hang the flesh of the future.
there remains little to be told.
they have lived this way since god created cattle,
and little remains to be told.

it is a relief to break the silence:
he watches her khanga unfold into daylight;
she assembles her welts, gathers her herd of pain,
bleeds death as she learns
to navigate
his world as he
navigates hers.
she will return from her post
in the evening,
roused.

yes, i sing your beauty

yes, i sing your beauty—how can i not sing your beauty?
your sky, slanted as politicians' lies,
promises fair weather—rainbows
dance over the ancestral remains,
these ramparts against skewed and twisted storms
where now only lies stone on stone.

the whitened skeleton of the earth laps the shores,
edges its way through the entrails: black blood flows
in these veins: this is just the beginning: a calligraphy of pain.

the woman of angra pequeña

on the beach, nothing remains:
her last words hammered against the rocks:
the ramparts of the stone kraal
strange as language on her lips.
words move from mouth to mouth —
revolution burns fierce in her,
the gradual turn of northern seasons
askew on her shoulders.

in the coffee shops and in the museum
bones and bones   and bones in messemb bay,
the earth splayed like a cheap whore
and in the veld, the wounded flower,
stunted arms held high.

can we ever forget:
cairns on the koppie at swartbooisdrift
cairns at angra pequeña
o god, caesar cassinga pomegranate red in my hand
raw as love for this land
in the blood water of dias
my love my wife my dove
we parse the grammar of our loins.

---

angra pequeña: A point just south of present-day Lüderitz where Bartholomeu
Dias is thought to have landed to erect a padrão (stone cross), and where some
surmise he dropped the 'dias woman.'

swartbooisdrift: A fording point west of the Epupa Falls along the Kunene River.
It is named after Petrus Swartbooi, a Nama leader who used the area as a base
for cattle raids. In 1881, the Dorsland Trekkers, a group of Afrikaners who settled
in Angola in the late nineteenth century, forded the river there. During the War
of Liberation, South African troops maintained an outpost at Swartbooisdrift to
prevent soldiers from the People's Liberation Army of Namibia, who were based
in Angola, from fording the river.

dragfoot stands on the rocks, bound to the firmament.
there is no record of his passing save the cry
of the wind erasing his tracks.
he yearns for his lover, this dark woman of dias.
far above her head
birds aim for the distance:
further and further and further between worlds
and dreams: home is where the entrails lie.
home is the hunter's stomach.
freedom follows the narrow road.
the coffle of skeletons
the soldiers lying in ambush on the beachhead
the offal of his bones.

dragfoot peddles along the paths of angra pequeña
pushes his wooden leg firmly against the earth
plucks the nasality of her voice
as it rises above the dunes.

the morning air is sharp against the dulled night air.
on the beach, nothing remains:
their last words beaten against the rocks,
the ramparts crumbling against the foreignness of the tongue.

the grey stone of memory rattles through the ages.
dragfoot caresses the stone in his hand, a piecework
hammered from the madness of a typewriter:
pecking birds peck
'cos peck peck pecks
holes in wounds.

hurt hangs in the air
the rhythm of their bodies
the dream-flecked smokiness of days
bubble over the horizon
words sweated from this earth.

such fragile soil, such wizened branches
such fleshy roots leaked into the permeable delta
of words coupling entrail to entrail.

he melts the words in his throat,
lets them emerge again thick as honey,
lashes their longing to the stem of the mopani.

scars as ancient as these hills of imagining,
premonitions blossoming
where mount etjo rises yellowed in springtime.

he enters her, feels the grip of her body
enclose him in an almost-forgotten memory.
she is slower and more generous than he recalls,
just the dull ache of bone and memory — he covets
the lost moments of her body against his,
her skin and the darkened wounds of her body.

after the dust settles

dragfoot pores over the tumbrelled entrails.
some days, words do not speak to him,
sometimes the drought of this desert pervades his mind.
months pass this way —
yii! the anguish!
eh! the heartstopped breath!
words settle like tumbrels against the desert
and a gemsbok searches for dew among the vygies:
monks spread like poems in the sand,
windswept as the woman of dias
on the shores at angra pequeña.

where are they, these windswept words?
where are they, these bitter dried naras
that rail against his frail body?

how do we speak the lingering pain?
how do we read
this strange alphabet,
arrange the clicks and sucks of death?
how do we write freedom in the blood of the entrails?
how do we write these darkened alleyways of blood
where the city crawls and groans?

at the shebeen, a woman stands.
at the shebeen, a woman falls.
freedom writes herself in words
flint as blood.

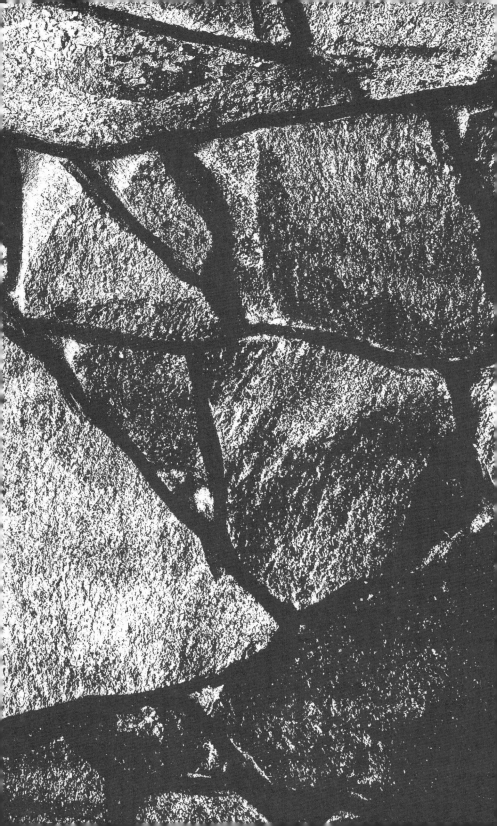

acknowledgements

Several of these poems have appeared in altered versions in other publications:

portions of 'things that get lost' appeared in *Unquiet Bones* (Wolsak & Wynn, 2015);

earlier versions of 'a history of dust,' 'the horses of hunger,' and 'petrel at daybreak' appeared in *Dark Victims*, a chapbook published by the Olive Reading Series;

a draft version of 'a heart should not beat like this' also appeared on the Canadian poetries website;

'words melt in his mouth' is included in *Wreaths for a Wayfarer: An Anthology in Honour of Pius Adesanmi* (Daraja Press, Montreal and Narrative Landscape Press, Lagos, Nigeria).

I am indebted to Jon Bridgman for the account of a killing he quotes in *The Revolt of the Hereros* (Berkeley and Los Angeles: University of California Press, 1981, p. 15) and which forms the basis of 'let us not think of them as barbarians' and also for Rev. Vedder's account of an Omuherero who had lived a traditional life (31–32).

The lines 'their breath knits them to this frozen world' in 'a heart should not beat like this' grew from a post on Philippa Yaa de Villiers's facebook page.

My thanks to all the early readers of these poems, in English and in Afrikaans. You know who you are. Know that the poems are better for your input. Louis Esterhuizen edited the Afrikaans version of this collection with extraordinary insight — his comments helped me make necessary revisions to both the English and Afrikaans versions. Jenna Butler, my editor at NeWest, edited the final manuscript with care and perceptiveness. I have no words to thank Juliane Okot Bitek for the afterword.

afterword: how to read calligraphies of sorrow

'you cannot write this down
you cannot create calligraphies of pain
says the singer of sorrows'

And so the poems reveal themselves. They are the palimpsests, and our job is to see what we can see, to read what we can read. These poems are sensuous; they evoke all our senses, get us to read the calligraphies through sight, touch, taste, hearing, and smell. But beyond the evocations, once we can read, what do we do with what we have? This collection is provocative; it does not try to tie up any loose ends. It does not attempt to placate, to solve, to live up to our expectations of who should be speaking, when and why and how. In these days, alight with debates of cultural appropriation, the gaze, identity politics and whiteness, these poems sound like a cacophony of voices, diverse ones, from different times, geographies and cultures. They are voices we rarely hear outside of footnotes and vignettes. Here, they are centralized and work to create a devastating collection by way of considering the legacy of colonialism in Namibia and the reverberations of the first genocide of the twentieth century, when the Germans attempted to exterminate the Ovaherero people. If these voices do not arise from the throats of those we imagine sing these 'songs of sorrows,' then what are we saying about our ability to read? Can we even read? Must we always look for the familiar? These poems do double work: they challenge what we think we know about the relationship between history and the present and ask us to consider what else would be going on. The poems demand that we reflect on how we come to knowledge, especially that which is not hegemonic but is definitely central to another world. How do our poems relate to poems from other centres, not ours? Must we have to fit, categorize, draw parallels? How do we hold space, make space, by which I want to say, how and when does our hospitality show? These poems begin with the epigraph 'you navigate the world differently after death' that sets us up in an afterlife. This makes me think: what was life like? The first account is one of the Herero describing the reality of life before death. It was normal — 'there's not much to be told' — it was the same way that it had always been, and in the 'not much to be told' is also the forgotten and disappeared — 'not much remains to be told.' Therefore, whatever we access will depend on our ability to read the ondjembo erose, to follow 'the gut of the cow.' These poems are a journey that doesn't depend on what we think we already know. In order for us to come away with anything, first, we must not 'think of them as barbarians,' and so we don't. And then we're set up for the devastating definition of what barbarians actually do, what words like genocide, mass killing, extermination don't do. These poems do two things in addressing the genocide against the Ovaherero:

I They hold us by our necks to the heat. Genocide, which can be understood to define the ultimate intention of colonialism, is more than theft of land and people, more than erasure of culture, more than exploitation on unimaginably grand scale, more than a smug response that that was those days, as if it ever ends. More than anything, it is the insistence of its culture and being as central in understanding what the world is. These poems underscore the resistance to all that. There was a world that did not and does not depend on the colonial paradigm. It centres itself and does not need to explain or translate itself. The revolution is not in the resistance but in its insistence on itself. So when the ritteltit dance is danced, it is nothing to do with how we understand women and women's bodies.

It is, if we're to understand the calligraphy, the confidence in the body that does not need a hero but knows itself to be one on whom the resistance depends. Women's bodies as resistance against colonialism, slavery, neo-colonial exploitation, and resistance movements is not much studied or centralised in a western imagination that is mostly patriarchal, not even in the contemporary ways of understanding feminism. This body does not need to be protected. It is not fragile. It is dignified in its hardness, in its defiance, and if you can't read that, then what else are you missing in reading the land?

2   They gesture toward an ontology that does not depend on any other while referencing other like ways of knowing. Recently, I watched Simon Gikandi's Yale keynote on the ALA conference on YouTube. He was parsing out (among other things) the difference and positioning of African and other world literatures. He talked about the world of literature as defined by the spaces in which literatures are consumed. So that Swahili poetry, by definition, is already world lit because it encompasses many worlds. It doesn't need to be read in English to be world lit. He also spoke of untranslateability as one of the ways that African literature insists on itself. It doesn't need to be translated to make sense. It is evidence of the failure of the genocide. There is still a world and being that exists, even with everything that was lost, and it still does not depend on the colonial centre. If there's a weakness in this collection, it's the attempt to translate. It reduces the tension of not knowing and frees the reader who should understand that the ability to read should not grant access to the whole story. There are some things that must remain unstranslated, but the gist comes across in the poetry. And it does. Dragfoot is an excellent example of the untranslated, but ondjembo is not.

Juliane Okot Bitek

To honour NeWest Press' 40th anniversary, we inaugurated a new poetry series to go alongside our Nunatak First Fiction, Prairie Play, and Writer as Critic series: Crow Said Poetry. Crow Said is named in honour of Robert Kroetsch's foundational 1977 novel *What The Crow Said*. The series aims to shed light on places and people outside of the literary mainstream. It is our intention that the poets featured in this series will continue Robert Kroetsch's literary tradition of innovation, interrogation, and generosity of spirit.

Peter Midgley is the author of several books of poetry, children's literature, and plays. He lives in Edmonton.